GOYLE, CHERT, MIRE

BY THE SAME AUTHOR

POETRY

Tattoos for Mother's Day
Hard Water
Tilt
Sleeping Keys
Green Noise

NON-FICTION

Strands
These Silent Mansions
Night Vision: In search of the true dark

GOYLE, CHERT, MIRE

Jean Sprackland

CAPE POETRY

1 3 5 7 9 10 8 6 4 2

Jonathan Cape, an imprint of Vintage, is part of the
Penguin Random House group of companies

Vintage, Penguin Random House UK, One Embassy Gardens,
8 Viaduct Gardens, London SW11 7BW

penguin.co.uk/vintage
global.penguinrandomhouse.com

First published by Jonathan Cape in 2026

Copyright © Jean Sprackland 2026

The moral right of the author has been asserted

Penguin Random House values and supports copyright. Copyright fuels creativity, encourages diverse voices, promotes freedom of expression and supports a vibrant culture. Thank you for purchasing an authorised edition of this book and for respecting intellectual property laws by not reproducing, scanning or distributing any part of it by any means without permission. You are supporting authors and enabling Penguin Random House to continue to publish books for everyone. No part of this book may be used or reproduced in any manner for the purpose of training artificial intelligence technologies or systems. In accordance with Article 4(3) of the DSM Directive 2019/790, Penguin Random House expressly reserves this work from the text and data mining exception.

Typeset in 11/13pt Bembo Book MT Pro by Six Red Marbles UK, Thetford, Norfolk
Printed and bound in Great Britain by TJ Books

The authorised representative in the EEA is Penguin Random House Ireland,
Morrison Chambers, 32 Nassau Street, Dublin D02 YH68

A CIP catalogue record for this book is available from the British Library

ISBN 9781787335912

Penguin Random House is committed to a sustainable future
for our business, our readers and our planet. This book is made
from Forest Stewardship Council® certified paper.

*for archaeologist Nan Pearce,
who over four decades collected thousands
of prehistoric stone artefacts from the fields
around her home in the Blackdown Hills*

CONTENTS

GOYLE   1

CHERT   19

MIRE   37

Notes & Acknowledgements   55

GOYLE

found in the dialects of Somerset and Devon; etymology unknown

Broken gate jammed across the ditch,
tied with rope so old it has become interesting
and you suddenly remember *art*.
Barbed wire, feed sack, rusty carburettor,
matted corpse, too big for crow.
This is the goyle bottom, the clogged
and leaf-logged anticlimactic place
where all loose items come to rest.
Occult among blackthorn and bramble,
an entry point for one who needs somewhere to be.
Squeeze through a gap by a wounded oak,
bark torn away down one flank
revealing the pulled meat inside.
Turn your back on the light and crawl in.

You will own this parcel of land,
said the solicitor (as if it came wrapped
and containing secrets). From *here* –
he clicked his propelling pencil – to *here*.
When you tried to pace it later, that line
was lost inside a hedge, wandered
over a stream and back again.
Still there was a goyle,
and that's a boundary, map or no map.
No one fights over a goyle.
But it is not a line on a map; it's a throat,
gouged out by flood, shut in from sky.
No place for human traffic.
Dank, trackless, mostly impassable.

Your house is a simple instrument
for the telling of weather. Wind pushes
at the front or at the back, playful or spiteful,
fingers the curtains as if to judge their quality.
An old door slams. From every tree a bird takes fright.
A dog at the farm makes five short barks in a row.
Dynamics of clouds: the way they slide
above and beneath, thicken and thin,
suck up colour and throw it down.
A window levered open between them,
just a crack at first, then wider, then a blaze of blue
that makes the blood move in your body.
You can lean out and feel that blue like a future.
You can lean and count until it slides shut.

You too have become an instrument
for the telling of weather:
watching yourself for signs,
lying awake and listening for changes.
The recent illness flares and settles inside you.
This is a place of quarantine,
the top road deserted now
except for a buzzard tearing at its kill.
There's sickness too in the world of the seedhead:
you turned one in your fingers
and saw it was stricken. And bees stagger
under the blue cowl of the monkshood,
sucking up sweetness and poison
in one dizzying draught.

Dusk starts early here, goes viral.
Wind rattles its keys in the locks.
Information rushes along the top road
and does not turn down the lane.
No use interrogating your screens –
they always show the same old answers.
Walk out of the house
and let their power drain to nothing.
As you go a helicopter tracks you
then loses you. And now the goyle
is the deep groove you think along.
Like this sprawling holly
where the sparrow enters
and follows its spiky logic, room to room.

How did the water eat so deep a channel,
now no more than a seep?
Cold sweat runs down the face of the wall.
Lick it: you'll find it sweet.
It runs into a basin of roots, lined with moss,
where the twisted feet of trees grip the sill.
You long to find – of course you do –
an arrowhead, potsherd or axe.
The goyle does hold these things.
But the past is so present,
your own life so compressed,
you barely exist here, and such a discovery
could wall up time. So inch forward,
looking and trying not to look.

What gods still have their congregations here
among these toppled statues, this makeshift altar?
Ferns unroll their green wisdom
over the charred scrolls of the earlier faith.
An ash lies waiting for sacrifice,
so like a beast in its thick fur of moss
you half expect to feel a heartbeat.
Lesion, necrosis, death of the crown –
the question spores from tree to tree
and no one knows how to answer it. Overhead
one branch strains against another
and you hear the groan of old hinges
as the wind shoves open the temple door,
glances inside, and moves on.

Blag Don, Hill of the Wolf.
This is where she dragged her kill
and left a few scattered bones.
This was a safe place to birth a litter,
sheltered from the blizzard. Here,
crouch in the dirt and look for prints
where she slinked in under the lintel,
muzzle stained with blood,
and took the water's right of way
to the valley floor and the river. Yes
eight hundred years have passed,
but these are the changed dynamics of time:
the way it slides, thickens and thins,
sucks up life and throws it down.

A drop swells on the lip of a leaf and falls
like a word being said, breaks in the green basin
and runs away not quite to nothing.
Then a small silence, before the next drop
gathers and speaks. Wait the silences
the way you used to wait between the chimes of a clock
as you crossed a square in some town or other,
listening for the bell to tip and swing on its yoke,
for the tongue to flex and utter its one word,
the only word in the language. This hour no different
from the hour just spent or squandered, this day like
every other, and each moment tending towards the next:
the toll of the bell, the dripping tap,
the footsteps echoing and draining away.

But that was another life.
Now the way darkens ahead.
Go under a prostrate branch
and over a high threshold
to a staircase of black roots.
An ash squats above you, like
an old king with robes hitched up.
Time too is propped on nothing,
parts seized with mud, could simply
fold with us inside it. Look -
on this dead branch the fungus
they call King Alfred's Cakes – just
a folk-name, like Shepherd's Purse,
Lady's Mantle, Cuckoo Spit –

But likeness collapses before your eyes.
They don't *resemble* cakes,
they *are* them, snatched from the fire
and flung through the open door
by a hard-pressed woman who doesn't know
he's the king, or doesn't care.
You useless bugger, can't you get anything right?
Yes, that must be it – whatever happened,
anytime, anywhere, is happening here, now –
Hush hush, you're tired. Get you out
from under the royal privy, look for somewhere
safe to rest. Ivy makes a good bed,
huge leaves supple as leather, glossy as hearts.
Ivy will work its enchantment.

You could be walled up
in this strange anchorage
where trees put down their roots in thin air
like something from a parable.
No one would think of looking for you here.
And there must be cures to be found
if only you knew where to look –
a green apothecary, a library
where the old recipes are kept.
Ropes of ivy drawn across the place,
a shawl of moss on every rope,
and tiny ferns lodged in the moss,
and water dripping from the ferns,
and pilgrim gnats attending the water.

Lock down, hold fast, hang on
like belts and buckles in the rental van
that kept your boxes safe
when you hit the brakes too hard
and skidded across the lane.
Or a vault, where certain items are stashed –
seeds, chemicals, quantities of gold.
Or a promise, requiring to be sworn and inked.
But illness has its own vitality
and spring will not be restrained
by straps or seals or signatures.
Its furniture slides and collides,
its volatile chemicals spill,
promises like apple blossom torched by frost.

Blackthorn winter
and on every thorn a bead of ice –
snow half-melted then refrozen –
is now snipped free
by the warmth of the day,
thawing and falling around you.
It looks like a shattering,
but it sounds like an unfolding,
like cellophane clenched into a ball
and dropped in a wastepaper basket,
where it slowly relaxes,
beginning, in that hopeless place,
to recover its true shape
and to speak of reprieve.

A green throat through which voices
are funnelled and mysteriously reversed:
the shriek of an owl in hunt,
a chainsaw, a fallen lamb.
A throat that swallows things too
and will swallow you, if you want.
You can lie hidden from the helicopter
and the moon with her blistered face
and the rookery blasted by gunshot.
Forget the house, the lane, the square —
lie on your bed of ivy till it's over.
Black fruits glowing in the rafters,
bees in the brain of the hollow log,
broken gate jammed across the ditch.

CHERT

*in former times these were known as the Scythe Stone Hills,
and full of antediluvian remains*

A woman walks the same field for forty years,
and the field speaks to her because it knows her.
She stops, picks up a word, and with quick eyes and hands
translates it. Knife. Arrowhead. Pick. Adze.
It's a vocation,
like sitting and listening while someone talks.
Pain worked to the surface, words shaped into tools.
The field itself brings them forth
from the utter dark of the deep self –
Oh rubbish, she thinks,
it's just walking and finding. She ought to stop.
The shelves are stacked with them. The cold gets in her hip.
But the field speaks, the pain outcrops,
and she bends to pick it up.

Not the delft blues of true flint,
nor the prussian blue of blue lias.
Not the glassy delicacy of quartz, but this
brown and white vernacular of waxy fracture,
knuckled and veined, charred and patched.
Struck with steel, it spits out a spark,
but in the local dialect.
Cropping at every step of the boot
and every cut of the spade
on the enclosure fields
behind the avenues of beech,
and the valley fields
that curve under ash and alder
and still answer to their old names.

They gathered scythestone at the head of the stream.
If there was any chert in it they chucked it —
chert was too hard, it ruined the blade.
But it was very good for roads
so women and children picked it from the fields
and paupers sat on the ground all day
and cracked it to size with a hammer.
Later they drove mines into the greensand.
The smeech the miners breathed
meant sickness in the lungs:
lesion, necrosis, early death. Still
it made a tolerable living while it lasted.
There are fields in these valleys still mown by scythe
and the chert road lies dreaming under the new road.

Thickset and serviceable,
like farmhouse crockery in a charity shop,
and in the same outmoded colours.
Hardwearing, hard to shift these days,
the kind of stuff your grandparents could afford
but not afford to lose. Who knows where it went
and where it is now, their cupboard full of cloam,
none of it matching, most of it chipped or crazed.
No end to the fields you'd have to search
to find the shattered pieces of yourself.
But look, under the hawthorn hedge,
surely that's the plate you loved as a child,
the one with the strange design of clouds
you gazed at so long it came to feel like a mirror.

At dusk it gives off a dim glow,
like those rags of foam
spun when the river is high.
At night from an upstairs window
you see it considered by moonlight:
it is at its most eloquent then.
But this is not the whole story –
when you walk the field
and bring back stones in your pocket
you bring back plastic too –
shreds of bright stuff,
dividing and dividing again
in their cellular determination to survive
over every timescale.

You saw this same kind in another life.
A field where you walked barefoot,
where drought had sucked the ground apart
into deep cracks you thought you might fall into,
and keep falling. The same kind –
but warm, cockled, flushed with pink light.
And you spread a towel, and lay down together,
with the navy-blue wood rearing up behind you.
The snapping of twigs, the reek of wild boar,
and somewhere the rumble of the combine harvester,
still out at sunset, heading your way.
Swigging from the bottle, and spitting cherry stones,
and gold leaf glittering on the farm roofs,
and someone saying Yes always, Yes I will.

Midsummer.
Birdsong stripped from the air's stems.
Down by the river the old house is scattered.
You stand and say their names
but there's no echo.
You clamber over the tumps and cairns,
walking and finding, but it's all
fish tins, clay pipes, brown bottles.
Under the rusty trees stones keep their mossy silence.
Language itself is prone to collapse, you think.
It's like an old house
where the rain gets in and ruins everything.
The walls sag, the ceilings cave,
one room of words falls through into another.

Garden wall with dreamwork of lichen,
so frank you remember *knowledge*.
You kneel on wet grass and try to read.
This part the colour of spilt milk,
the form like bones on an X-ray, a bluewhite
diagram of choice and consequence
seen to be infinite. But what have these
cool pale logic-puzzles to do with
the rough brown shag that neighbours them,
cheerfully pubic? And what kinship
with this third kind, like a cache
of leather casks strung on red cord?
(Containing, they say, a store of wine so ancient
it would draw speech to any forgetful mouth.)

Pinched blooms, sap drained from the gland.
Late buds like stopped mouths.
Behind a screen of thorns
a bird describes the pouring of water,
stops to draw from the source, and pours again.
Leaf hands splayed and crabbed
make gestures to be guessed at.
Sun touches them, and they curl
as hands once curled in speech.
Underbrush of brittling stems, soon to be cut down
yet still giving forth a green that is composite –
bruised blues, medicinal pinks,
sickroom yellows, dirty-sheet whites
all meet in the late green of this giving forth.

To build a new house you must begin
by walking the field
and picking up stones.
You must heave and heap them,
barrow them over carr,
drag them through mire,
chuck them and stack them
till your hands bleed. You need *thousands* –
but the field will not miss them
any more than you miss the words you spoke.
They were on the air, and gone.
Too late to call them back,
too far to find the place.
So start again, start again.

In the quiet lanes of the parietal lobe
the illness has installed a truckload
of listening equipment, set to scan
for everything everywhere all the time.
Birds massing along a border, perhaps,
or the priming and loading of ominous silences.
You're picking up static, said the doctor,
white noise outside the range of hearing.
It's just the phantom sound of attention,
she said, like lying awake at night
(have you ever done this, I wonder?)
listening to someone breathing, alert to any change,
so slight it might be a moth on the sheet,
or a distant power turning its fire on another.

Beyond the range of human hearing
a distant power turns its fire on another.
It shivers the surface of this brown pool
and the small dead lie where they fall,
becoming inscrutable in the mud:
wrist of oak sleeved in moss;
derelict snail; kit for building a spider;
insect wing cut from a sheet of bridal silk
and still bearing the scissormarks.
All was done with care, and all were loved –
you see this clearly in their decomposing.
Also in the aftermath of smashed stone:
here a trace of gold lustre,
there a thumbprint or a maker's mark.

These high winds are a ruthless tactic
to clear out the remnants of summer.
Branches, leaves, the last of the year's fruit,
lichen dry as the hair of a corpse –
everything must go.
Put on your boots and your big coat
which smells of last year's bonfires
and go out looking for microliths.
On the hill the gorse has been razed to ash.
By the river, a pheasant opened
and tossed like last season's brochure.
Ah, but it's grand to be out in the wind
where chert takes its autumn forms
of broken antler, cattle bone and spoilt meat.

Illness has scrambled the year.
Midwinter, and the ground is white with frost
yet the oak across the field is in leaf –
No, look again, those leaves are starlings,
and listen, their noise is the noise
of meltwater hurtling over stones,
uprooting and flinging them downstream.
Smoke rises from the white grass.
There will be thaw. The stream will run like milk.
Despite all losses you are still alive. Now
the tree shakes out its leaves, the sky tumbles with ash
and that thump in your chest
is the bolt being thrown
as the year lurches open on the heart's old hinges.

A woman walks the same river for forty days.
She comes here to recover.
Underfoot the bed of chert. Under it, greensand. Under it, ooze.
The stones bear tiny figures,
most too small to see: Diatom. Radiolarian.
Sometimes a suggestion of texture: comb, feather.
So this is meaning, she thinks. Minor bodies
in their millions, scuttled and sinking, becoming sediment.
Day and night collaborate on the difficult work of translation.
Stars flare and fade. Ice swells and shrinks.
Diagenesis. Lithification.
Now the river brings them forth
from the utter dark of the deep self.
She stops, picks up a word.

MIRE

the slow self-inhumation and self-resurrection of the bog

All day a buzzard calls over the mire,
like the desperate note of a whistle
blown by a search party. You are marooned
on quag and quaking bog - a dark
anoxic brew of mud and dead matter.
The water table rises, busts its underground cells
and repossesses the house.
It oozes up through the kitchen floor
and pools between flagstones
with a sheen of tannins and the rusty smell of blood
like something loosed from a sump
or dumped on a verge up the lane.
The carpet rots, the walls slough their plaster
and white salts stand up like hoarfrost on the sill.

You came to live on the springline
thinking that because you are made of water
you would understand this place.
Silvery water, falling like loosed hair,
sweet water, drawn from your own spring.
Summer shimmering over the wet grass,
dragonflies drinking at your footprints.
The fairytale river shuffling its deck of stones,
spinning its debris into foam,
leaping at low branches and biting them off.
But what about these long unnavigable days
when the house becomes a boat,
bilgy and listing, and the lane
bucks and writhes in its smooth brown pelt?

They have no value, said the agent,
spreading his empty hands on the desk,
wet places, these waste places.
Through all of history they have been
unproductive, useless for cultivation
or construction. Oh you can try attrition:
dig a drain and coax the water
from here to there, break your back
to gain a few yards of mud –
it floods back in as if it were tidal. No,
he said (with a glance at his watch),
I'd forget it if I were you. These barren places
are only fit to be fenced off, written off,
cursed, or wished away.

Archaeobotanist, anthrocologist,
palynologist, paleoentomologist:
all come with their various petitions,
all kneel and name what they seek:
God of the mire, grant us artefact, ecofact,
furnace, cesspit, midden and posthole.
Grant us charcoal, pollen, seed and shell,
thorax, femur, antler, tooth.
Then each scoops a reeking sample
to be judged in a tank of clean water:
all things float or sink, all are sieved or strained,
and under the glare of the laboratory lights
bear witness to what happened when:
flooding, burning, felling, famine, plague.

If you stand at the edge of the mire
where rushes raise their tattered flags
you might see the women of this house
stepping barefoot between brown pools,
cutting the stalks for their lamps.
Each to be trimmed and dipped in a dish of tallow,
plant and animal fused and held to the flame,
releasing the stink of mud and sheep,
spreading a quivering circle of light
where their quick hands spool the thread.
You might hear their tread where the stairs once turned,
before the fire that took the roof, as they carry
that glowing something-and-nothing
into creaking and rustling rooms.

Alder puts down its roots in mud,
grows fast and dies young.
A sombre tree, brooding on its losses.
They used to make clogs from the wood
for lime burners working at the kiln –
it was soft when cut, flushed with red sap,
easy to work and hardened as it cured.
Now it seeds and spreads where no one goes,
haunts the trackless and shadowy seclusion
of carr and turbary. Slither down the bank
to see the leafbuds glowing purple in the dusk.
Could you coppice it. Could you learn to make clogs.
You lop a broken branch and watch the wound,
pale at first, quickly stained with blood.

To take a core of mud from the springline mire
you need a chambered or Russian sampler.
Insert the sampler in the closed position
then turn the handle clockwise, to cut
a semi-cylinder with the sharpened bore.
Now turn counterclockwise to extrude it
without contamination by overlying sediments.
Back in the lab, begin the pollen count,
adding an aliquot of exotic spore for comparison,
then mount your samples in silicon oil
and magnify five hundred times.
Quercus, Alnus, Corylus, Fraximus, Salix.
There, under your lens, eleven thousand years
swim into focus looking much like now.

Of course there are some that prefer
the silky obscurity of mire,
its ambiguities, refusals, mongrel ways:
those with bespoke arrangements
like breathable skin, or multiple hearts,
those who can taste light, or walk on water,
brew their own poisons, carry their eggs in a rucksack,
hermaphrodites, and some that can enter
a temporary state of death when they need to.
But today they are bycatch –
it's the pollen you want. Now
the slim core is drawn to the surface
and behind it the sucking sound
of all the wet valves closing.

It's not like drilling into rock.
More like gentling with a silver instrument
through the soft matter of the hippocampus,
probing deeper, finding its way between
fish tins, clay pipes, brown bottles,
rags of sacking spored with smallpox,
pieces of wooden trackway where we walked
barefoot from one dry island to the next,
nudging aside the figured chert,
going right to the edge
of autobiographical memory,
then under the glare of the theatre lights
turning to your assistant and exclaiming
So many losses, yet we are still alive.

The illness pressed at one wet valve,
then another, and another,
trying its luck until it sprang a lock.
It forded the subarachnoid space,
knifed a hole in the pia mater, and was in,
roaming the salons and sculleries of the brain,
looking for things to break.
Petty vandalism, nothing more –
words melted over a flame,
wiring torn from time cells
and dumped in the optic chasm.
Nothing that couldn't be survived.
All day a buzzard calls over the mire
like the scream of someone waiting to be found.

Black pages glued together
are fished out and fingered and
magnified five hundred times
You packed your old diaries in
a shoe box packed the shoe box
in another box and then
strapped it all over with tape
Now the historian with
her careful hands is peeling
the pages apart taking
photographs checking dates and
there are the bad sentences
no one was meant to read and
the ghastly illustrations

But now from the floating house comes a voice
lifting a string of beads and touching them
in the order the gods require.
Forties, Cromarty, Forth and Tyne,
Dogger to German Bight by way of Fisher.
Fore cast, the line of the mind
baited and thrown into the heaving future.
There may be nowhere to go
but there is always this: listening in the dark,
adrift on a craft built from toothpicks
and tweezered through the neck of a bottle.
Northeasterly backing northerly, three to five.
No rift in the waves to show your passage,
no change of dialect among the gulls.

The lane would fill with snow and the postman
would walk the hedgetops to make his deliveries.
Now it rains instead, all winter long.
The mire sequesters its carbon,
sequesters its darkness, its long cool silence.
On the turbaries the peat was cut
for the poor man's fire, but now
those places are set aside for the hiker
in over the tops of her boots.
Sequester: to isolate, or hide away.
Sequestrate: to take possession
until a debt has been paid
or other claims have been made.
Confiscate. Declare bankrupt.

Lean out at the window – feel
the blood move in your body –
In another place and time
a rag of life snagged on you –
like a rag of river foam
blown on a rogue gust of wind –
It clings to you still – it thrills
with light – you cannot keep it –
but lean out again – feel that
blaze of blue like a future –
Life snagged on you – nothing but
spindrift plucked from the river –
A beautiful accident –
The wind has not freed it yet –

Sundew primes its red traps
for the keeled skimmer
with his gold and latticework
and the pearl-bordered fritillary
fresh from her natal feast of marsh violet.
Sphagnum mosses drink in draught after draught,
swell into hummocks, spread into rafts
where sedge flings out
its extravagant plumes of seed.
Underground, the mire preserves its dead,
guarding its acids, locking out oxygen,
starting the long translation from gley to peat.
Overhead, nightjar and warbler
test their stuttering machines.

NOTES & ACKNOWLEDGEMENTS

GOYLE

Monkshood is a beautiful but highly toxic aconite, also known as wolfsbane.

A blackthorn winter is a spell of unusually cold weather in early spring.

CHERT

Blue lias is a distinctive type of stone, found elsewhere in the region, and prized as a building material for its versatility and aesthetic quality.

'Cloam' is a west country word for earthenware or crockery.

The dialect word 'smeech' refers to dense, acrid smoke, fumes or dust.

A microlith is a stone tool, typically made of flint or chert.

The radiolarian (a microscopic marine organism) and the diatom (a single-celled alga) are both found in the fossil record, and provide evidence of environmental and climatic change over time.

'Lithification' and 'diagenesis' describe processes in the transformation of sediment into sedimentary rock, which can take millions of years to complete.

MIRE

The springline is the line where permeable greensand and impermeable clay sub-soils meet. Water is squeezed out sideways, and springs flow continually, creating areas of permanently wet ground.

Carr is wet woodland, typically dominated by alder or willow.

A turbary was a place on common ground where peat could be cut for fuel. There are several old turbaries in the Blackdowns, now managed as wildlife reserves.

In chemistry, the term 'aliquot' refers to a precise portion of a liquid or solid substance.

The pia mater is the innermost membrane surrounding the brain.

Gley is a sticky, water-logged soil, anoxic or lacking in oxygen.

*

I am grateful to the editors of the following publications in which some of these poems (or earlier versions of them) first appeared:

Place 2020, *The Tablet*, *Poetry London* and *The Poetry Review*.

The epigraph for 'Chert' is taken from *The Chronicles of Twyford* by F.J. Snell.

The epigraph for 'Mire' is taken from *Connemara: Listening to the Wind* by Tim Robinson.

Thank you to Robin Robertson and everyone at Cape; and to all those who supported and encouraged me through the illness and the writing of these poems, including my friends and colleagues at Manchester Metropolitan University.

Special thanks to Nigel, who knows the place.